This is _____'s plan for Ramadan year _____

Ramadan goals
Part 2

Family & friends

Relationship with family

Relationship with friends
- Being cooperative and kind.
- Helping them out.
- Supporting and advising them.

Parents
- Obeying them.
- Putting a smile on their face.
- Helping around the house.

Relatives
- Upholding continuous contact with them.
- Making them happy.

Siblings
- Being cooperative and kind.
- Helping them out.
- Supporting and advising them.

Ramadan goals
Part 3

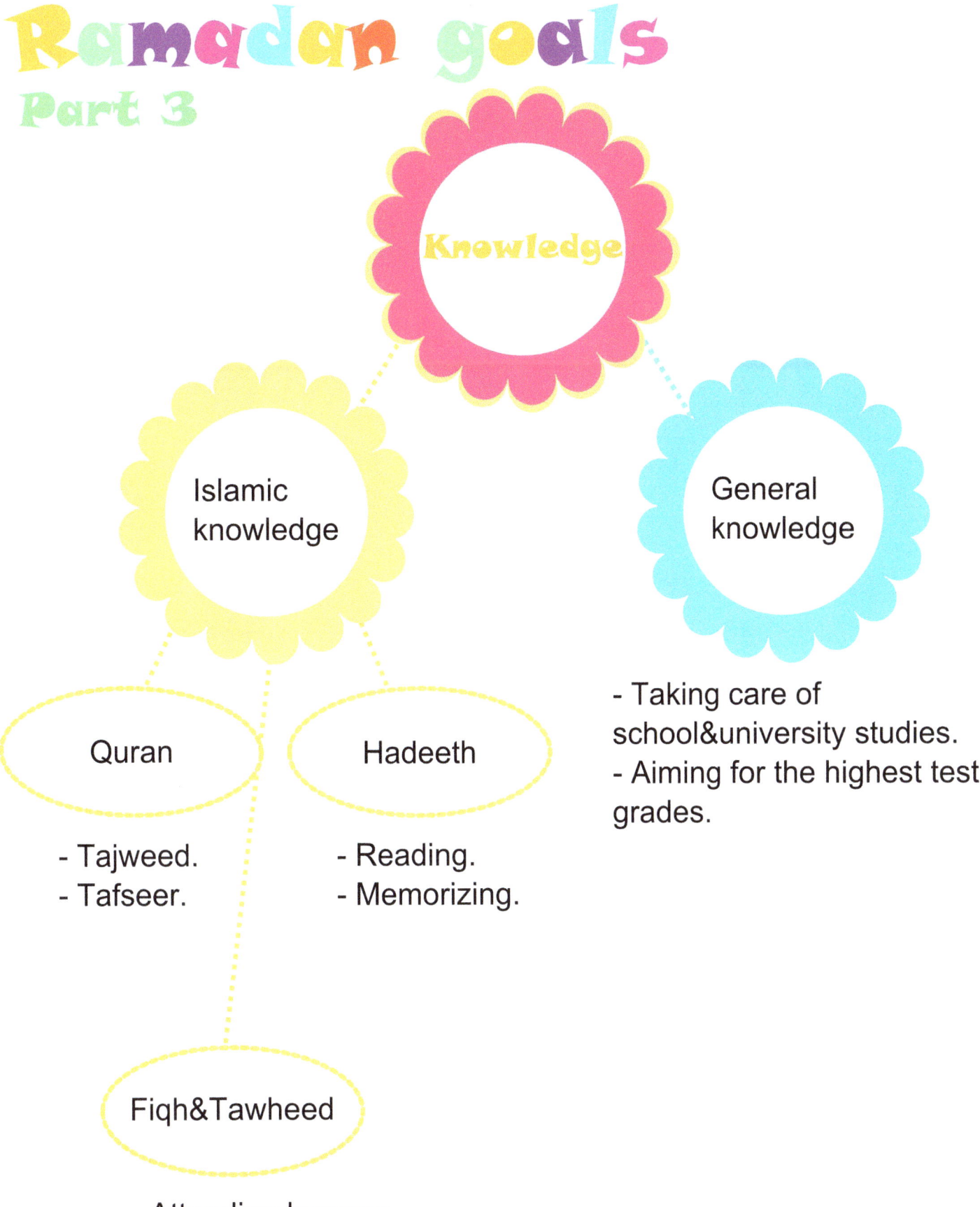

Ramadan goals
Part 4

Health & fitness

Food
- Not overeating, eating enough for sufficient energy.
- Eating healthy food.
- Making iftar with 3 dates or water to follow the sunnah.
- Not over spending on food.

Exercise
- Performing sport activity 3 days a week.
- Walking for 30 min daily.

Charity
- Putting aside a small amount of money to give out daily.
- Feeding people in need as much as possible.
- Making charity by smiling in people's faces and making beautiful Islamic greetings.
- Giving out more money in the last 10 days.
- Visiting orphanages, elderly homes, hospitals..etc.
- Giving away unwanted clothes and other belongings to people in need.

Look around you stop and stare

Who keeps the birds up in the air?
And who stops the sky from crashing down,
And keeps the earth spinning round.
Who orders the moon to come out at night?
To give us all a guiding light.
And order the night to give way to day
So the sun can warm us with her rays.
Who lets the rain from heaven fall down?
So the earth can bring forth from its ground,
Its herbs, its spices and its vegetables
Its fruits and other things edible.
Sour, salty, bitter and sweet,
So many delicious things for us to eat
Look around you stop and stare,
Can't you see the signs everywhere?
Who made all living things, so many kinds?
The insects, the animals and even mankind.
Some so tiny and small like ants or flees
Others as big and tall as the trees,
Some slither and slide, swim or crawl,
While others run, fly or walk straight and tall.
Every creature knows its place where it should be
On land, in the air or under the sea
Each type of creature has its own name
Each one unique no two are the same
Who should we give thanks to all this for
Allah, the only one, the creator.

By Aisha Abdel Rahman

Allah is the most merciful. He has more mercy on you and more love for you than anyone in the world including your parents.
His mercy is for everyone, go to Him and you will not be turned away.
Use the to do list in the next page to write down your main goals and dreams in these special days. And especially what you want to achieve in each area such as how much Quran you want to read daily, how many hadiths you want to read..etc
And don't forget to write down your special duaa's.

Heaven gates are open wide

Beautiful green gardens no end can be reached
With pure clear rivers flowing underneath
Everything cool and shaded by the canopy of the trees
Upon your face you feel a gentle breeze
By gentle flowing rivers are magnificent mansions
For you to live in with pure and holy companions
The people's faces beam brightly with bliss
Wearing pearl necklaces and gold bracelets upon their wrists
And garments of green brocade and silk is their dress
Rich carpets all spread out and cushions set in rows
You'll recline with dignity on raised thrones
Delicious drink and fruit served to you on gold and silver trays
Everything you desire is just a thought away
A heavenly scent of musk fills the air
Its aroma follows you everywhere
Hear the melodic notes of the choirs of angels
Singing to Allah songs of glory and praises
No war, hatred or jealousy
No hunger, thirst or poverty
Everyone living in peace, and serenity
Forever and ever for eternity
This is Heaven and it's waiting for us

Heaven gates are open wide

To live eternally in Paradise
The key to Heaven's gates are in your hands
To live by Allah's words in The Holy Quran
To believe in Allah the only one
He was not begotten nor has he a son
To believe in his prophet Mohammed
(May peace and blessings be him upon)
And follow his teachings and traditions
To pray to Allah five times a day
At special times and in a special way
To fast in the month of Ramadan
From when the sun rises to when it goes down
To pay the Zakat a tax on the rich and the wealthy
And give it to the poor and the needy
To visit Mecca for a pilgrimage
Wear special clothes and perform Hajj
If you do all this then you have the key
To live with Allah for eternity.

By Aisha Abdel Rahman

Day 1 — Write down the main things you did in each area

Prayer	Obligatory prayers	Sunan prayers	Tarwaeeh prayers	Night prayers
Quran	Daily reading		Memorizing	
Duaa&zikr	Special duaa's for Ramadan	Morning&evening azkaar		Filling time with zikr
Fasting	No food or drink	Dua'a at iftar	Keeping tongue pure	Iftar&suhoor at best times
Ethics	Honesty&integrity	Only saying good words	Helping others	Working hard
Parents	Obeying them	Putting a smile on their face	Helping around the house	
Relatives	Upholding continuous contact with them		Making them happy	
Siblings	Being cooperative&kind	Helping them out	Supporting&advising them	
Friends	Being cooperative&kind	Helping them out	Supporting&advising them	
Food	Not overeating	Eating healthy food	Break fast with 3 dates/water	
Exercise	Walking for 30 min daily		Performing sport activity 3 days a week	
Charity				

Areas I need to improve

Narrated by Sahl the prophet (peace be upon him) said "There is a gate in Paradise called Ar-Raiyan, and those who observe fasts will enter through it on the Day of Resurrection and none except them will enter through it. It will be said, 'Where are those who used to observe fasts?' They will get up, and none except them will enter through it. After their entry the gate will be closed and nobody will enter through it."

Sahih Bukhari Book 31 Hadith 120

Day 2 — Write down the main things you did in each area

Prayer	Obligatory prayers	Sunan prayers	Tarwaeeh prayers	Night prayers
Quran	Daily reading		Memorizing	
Duaa&zikr	Special duaa's for Ramadan	Morning&evening azkaar	Filling time with zikr	
Fasting	No food or drink	Dua'a at iftar	Keeping tongue pure	Iftar&suhoor at best times
Ethics	Honesty&integrity	Only saying good words	Helping others	Working hard
Parents	Obeying them	Putting a smile on their face	Helping around the house	
Relatives	Upholding continuous contact with them		Making them happy	
Siblings	Being cooperative&kind	Helping them out	Supporting&advising them	
Friends	Being cooperative&kind	Helping them out	Supporting&advising them	
Food	Not overeating	Eating healthy food	Break fast with 3 dates/water	
Exercise	Walking for 30 min daily		Performing sport activity 3 days a week	
Charity				

Something significant I learned today

Special events that happened today

"Ramadan is the (month) in which the Quran was sent down, as a guide to mankind and a clear guidance and judgment (so that mankind will distinguish from right and wrong)"

The Holy Quran, Chapter 2 verse 183

Day 3 — Write down the main things you did in each area

Prayer	Obligatory prayers	Sunan prayers	Tarwaeeh prayers	Night prayers
Quran	Daily reading		Memorizing	
Duaa&zikr	Special duaa's for Ramadan	Morning&evening azkaar	Filling time with zikr	
Fasting	No food or drink	Dua'a at iftar	Keeping tongue pure	Iftar&suhoor at best times
Ethics	Honesty&integrity	Only saying good words	Helping others	Working hard
Parents	Obeying them	Putting a smile on their face	Helping around the house	
Relatives	Upholding continuous contact with them		Making them happy	
Siblings	Being cooperative&kind	Helping them out	Supporting&advising them	
Friends	Being cooperative&kind	Helping them out	Supporting&advising them	
Food	Not overeating	Eating healthy food	Break fast with 3 dates/water	
Exercise	Walking for 30 min daily		Performing sport activity 3 days a week	
Charity				

Areas I need to improve

_____
_____
_____
_____
_____
_____

"Narrated by Ibn 'Abbas: The Prophet (peace be upon him) was the most generous amongst the people, and he used to be more so in the month of Ramadan when Gabriel visited him, and Gabriel used to meet him on every night of Ramadan till the end of the month. The Prophet used to recite the Holy Qur'an to Gabriel, and when Gabriel met him, he used to be more generous than a fast wind (which causes rain and welfare)."
Sahih Bukhari Book 31 Hadith 126

Day 4 — Write down the main things you did in each area

Prayer	Obligatory prayers	Sunan prayers	Tarwaeeh prayers	Night prayers
Quran	Daily reading		Memorizing	
Duaa&zikr	Special duaa's for Ramadan	Morning&evening azkaar		Filling time with zikr
Fasting	No food or drink	Dua'a at iftar	Keeping tongue pure	Iftar&suhoor at best times
Ethics	Honesty&integrity	Only saying good words	Helping others	Working hard
Parents	Obeying them	Putting a smile on their face	Helping around the house	
Relatives	Upholding continuous contact with them		Making them happy	
Siblings	Being cooperative&kind	Helping them out	Supporting&advising them	
Friends	Being cooperative&kind	Helping them out	Supporting&advising them	
Food	Not overeating	Eating healthy food	Break fast with 3 dates/water	
Exercise	Walking for 30 min daily		Performing sport activity 3 days a week	
Charity				

Something significant I learned today

Special events that happened today

"Fasting is prescribed for you as it was prescribed for those before you, that you may attain taqwaa (piety)."

The Holy Quran, Chapter 2 verse 183

Day 5 — Write down the main things you did in each area

Prayer	Obligatory prayers	Sunan prayers	Tarwaeeh prayers	Night prayers
Quran	Daily reading		Memorizing	
Duaa&zikr	Special duaa's for Ramadan	Morning&evening azkaar		Filling time with zikr
Fasting	No food or drink	Dua'a at iftar	Keeping tongue pure	Iftar&suhoor at best times
Ethics	Honesty&integrity	Only saying good words	Helping others	Working hard
Parents	Obeying them	Putting a smile on their face	Helping around the house	
Relatives	Upholding continuous contact with them		Making them happy	
Siblings	Being cooperative&kind	Helping them out	Supporting&advising them	
Friends	Being cooperative&kind	Helping them out	Supporting&advising them	
Food	Not overeating	Eating healthy food	Break fast with 3 dates/water	
Exercise	Walking for 30 min daily		Performing sport activity 3 days a week	
Charity				

Areas I need to improve

_____
_____
_____
_____
_____

"Narrated by Abu Huraira The Prophet (peace be upon him) said, "Whoever does not give up forged speech and evil actions, Allah is not in need of his leaving his food and drink (i.e. Allah will not accept his fasting.)"

Sahih Bukhari Book 31 Hadith 127

Day 6 — Write down the main things you did in each area

Prayer	Obligatory prayers	Sunan prayers	Tarwaeeh prayers	Night prayers
Quran	Daily reading		Memorizing	
Duaa&zikr	Special duaa's for Ramadan	Morning&evening azkaar		Filling time with zikr
Fasting	No food or drink	Dua'a at iftar	Keeping tongue pure	Iftar&suhoor at best times
Ethics	Honesty&integrity	Only saying good words	Helping others	Working hard
Parents	Obeying them	Putting a smile on their face	Helping around the house	
Relatives	Upholding continuous contact with them		Making them happy	
Siblings	Being cooperative&kind	Helping them out	Supporting&advising them	
Friends	Being cooperative&kind	Helping them out	Supporting&advising them	
Food	Not overeating	Eating healthy food	Break fast with 3 dates/water	
Exercise	Walking for 30 min daily		Performing sport activity 3 days a week	
Charity				

Something significant I learned today

Special events that happened today

"Narrated by Abu Huraira I heard Allah's Apostle (peace be upon him) saying regarding Ramadan, "Whoever prayed at night in it (the month of Ramadan) out of sincere Faith and hoping for a reward from Allah, then all his previous sins will be forgiven." Sahih Bukhari Book 31 Hadith 127

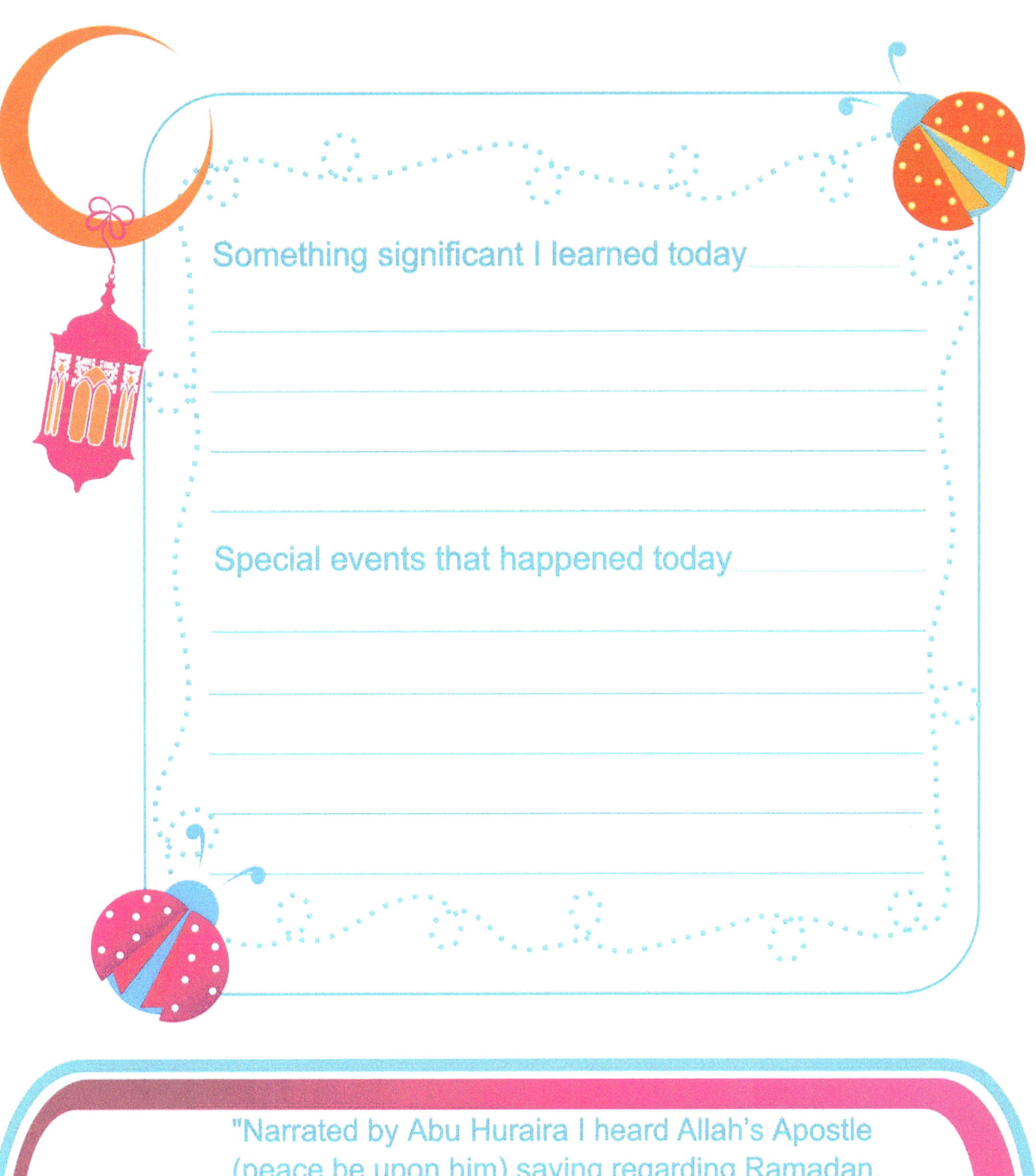

Day 7 — Write down the main things you did in each area

Prayer	Obligatory prayers	Sunan prayers	Tarwaeeh prayers	Night prayers
Quran	Daily reading		Memorizing	
Duaa&zikr	Special duaa's for Ramadan	Morning&evening azkaar	Filling time with zikr	
Fasting	No food or drink	Dua'a at iftar	Keeping tongue pure	Iftar&suhoor at best times
Ethics	Honesty&integrity	Only saying good words	Helping others	Working hard
Parents	Obeying them	Putting a smile on their face	Helping around the house	
Relatives	Upholding continuous contact with them		Making them happy	
Siblings	Being cooperative&kind	Helping them out	Supporting&advising them	
Friends	Being cooperative&kind	Helping them out	Supporting&advising them	
Food	Not overeating	Eating healthy food	Break fast with 3 dates/water	
Exercise	Walking for 30 min daily		Performing sport activity 3 days a week	
Charity				

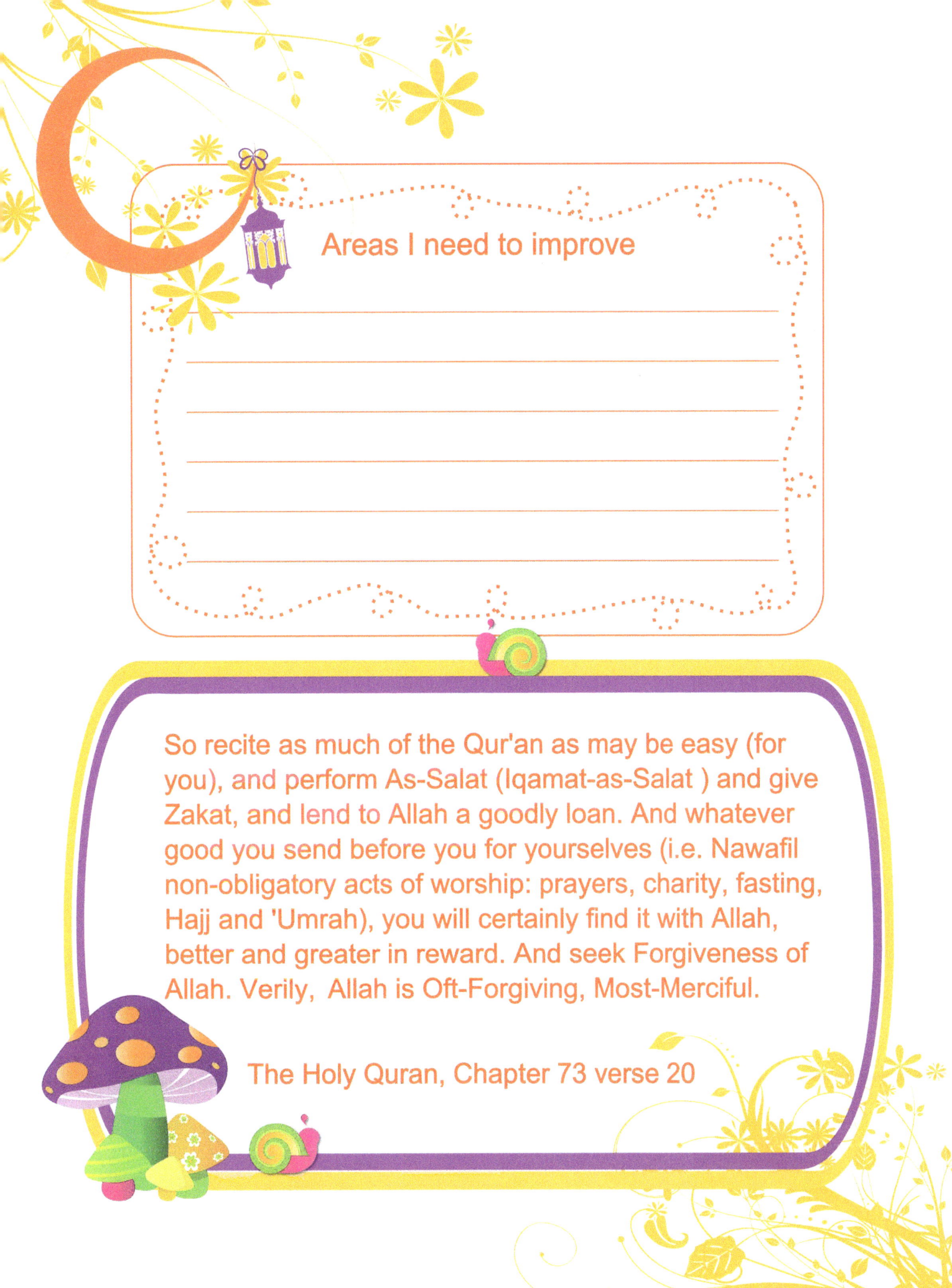

Areas I need to improve

_____
_____
_____
_____
_____
_____

So recite as much of the Qur'an as may be easy (for you), and perform As-Salat (Iqamat-as-Salat) and give Zakat, and lend to Allah a goodly loan. And whatever good you send before you for yourselves (i.e. Nawafil non-obligatory acts of worship: prayers, charity, fasting, Hajj and 'Umrah), you will certainly find it with Allah, better and greater in reward. And seek Forgiveness of Allah. Verily, Allah is Oft-Forgiving, Most-Merciful.

The Holy Quran, Chapter 73 verse 20

Day 8 — Write down the main things you did in each area

Area				
Prayer	Obligatory prayers	Sunan prayers	Tarwaeeh prayers	Night prayers
Quran	Daily reading		Memorizing	
Duaa&zikr	Special duaa's for Ramadan		Morning&evening azkaar	Filling time with zikr
Fasting	No food or drink	Dua'a at iftar	Keeping tongue pure	Iftar&suhoor at best times
Ethics	Honesty&integrity	Only saying good words	Helping others	Working hard
Parents	Obeying them	Putting a smile on their face	Helping around the house	
Relatives	Upholding continuous contact with them		Making them happy	
Siblings	Being cooperative&kind	Helping them out	Supporting&advising them	
Friends	Being cooperative&kind	Helping them out	Supporting&advising them	
Food	Not overeating	Eating healthy food	Break fast with 3 dates/water	
Exercise	Walking for 30 min daily		Performing sport activity 3 days a week	
Charity				

Something significant I learned today

Special events that happened today

Sahl b. Sa'd (Allah be pleased with him) reported Allah's Messenger (may peace be upon him) as saying: "The people will continue to prosper as long as they hasten the breaking of the fast."

Sahih Muslim Book 6 Hadith 2417

Day 9 — Write down the main things you did in each area

Area				
Prayer	Obligatory prayers	Sunan prayers	Tarwaeeh prayers	Night prayers
Quran	Daily reading		Memorizing	
Duaa&zikr	Special duaa's for Ramadan	Morning&evening azkaar		Filling time with zikr
Fasting	No food or drink	Dua'a at iftar	Keeping tongue pure	Iftar&suhoor at best times
Ethics	Honesty&integrity	Only saying good words	Helping others	Working hard
Parents	Obeying them	Putting a smile on their face	Helping around the house	
Relatives	Upholding continuous contact with them		Making them happy	
Siblings	Being cooperative&kind	Helping them out	Supporting&advising them	
Friends	Being cooperative&kind	Helping them out	Supporting&advising them	
Food	Not overeating	Eating healthy food	Break fast with 3 dates/water	
Exercise	Walking for 30 min daily		Performing sport activity 3 days a week	
Charity				

Areas I need to improve

_____
_____
_____
_____
_____
_____

Narrated by Abu Said Al-Khudri the Prophet (peace be upon him) said, "Amongst the men of Bani Israel there was a man who had murdered ninety-nine persons. Then he set out asking (whether his repentance could be accepted or not). He came upon a monk and asked him if his repentance could be accepted. The monk replied in the negative and so the man killed him. He kept on asking till a man advised to go to such and such village. (So he left for it) but death overtook him on the way. While dying, he turned his chest towards that village (where he had hoped his repentance would be accepted), and so the angels of mercy and the angels of punishment quarrelled amongst themselves regarding him. Allah ordered the village (towards which he was going) to come closer to him, and ordered the village (whence he had come), to go far away, and then He ordered the angels to measure the distances between his body and the two villages. So he was found to be one span closer to the village (he was going to). So he was forgiven."

Sahih Bukhari Book 56, Hadith 676

Day 10 — Write down the main things you did in each area

Area				
Prayer	Obligatory prayers	Sunan prayers	Tarwaeeh prayers	Night prayers
Quran	Daily reading		Memorizing	
Duaa&zikr	Special duaa's for Ramadan	Morning&evening azkaar	Filling time with zikr	
Fasting	No food or drink	Dua'a at iftar	Keeping tongue pure	Iftar&suhoor at best times
Ethics	Honesty&integrity	Only saying good words	Helping others	Working hard
Parents	Obeying them	Putting a smile on their face	Helping around the house	
Relatives	Upholding continuous contact with them		Making them happy	
Siblings	Being cooperative&kind	Helping them out	Supporting&advising them	
Friends	Being cooperative&kind	Helping them out	Supporting&advising them	
Food	Not overeating	Eating healthy food	Break fast with 3 dates/water	
Exercise	Walking for 30 min daily		Performing sport activity 3 days a week	
Charity				

Something significant I learned today

Special events that happened today

Narrated by Ibn Masud I heard the Prophet (peace be upon him) saying, "There is no envy except in two: a person whom Allah has given wealth and he spends it in the right way, and a person whom Allah has given wisdom (i.e. religious knowledge) and he gives his decisions accordingly and teaches it to the others."
Sahih Bukhari Book 24 Hadith 490

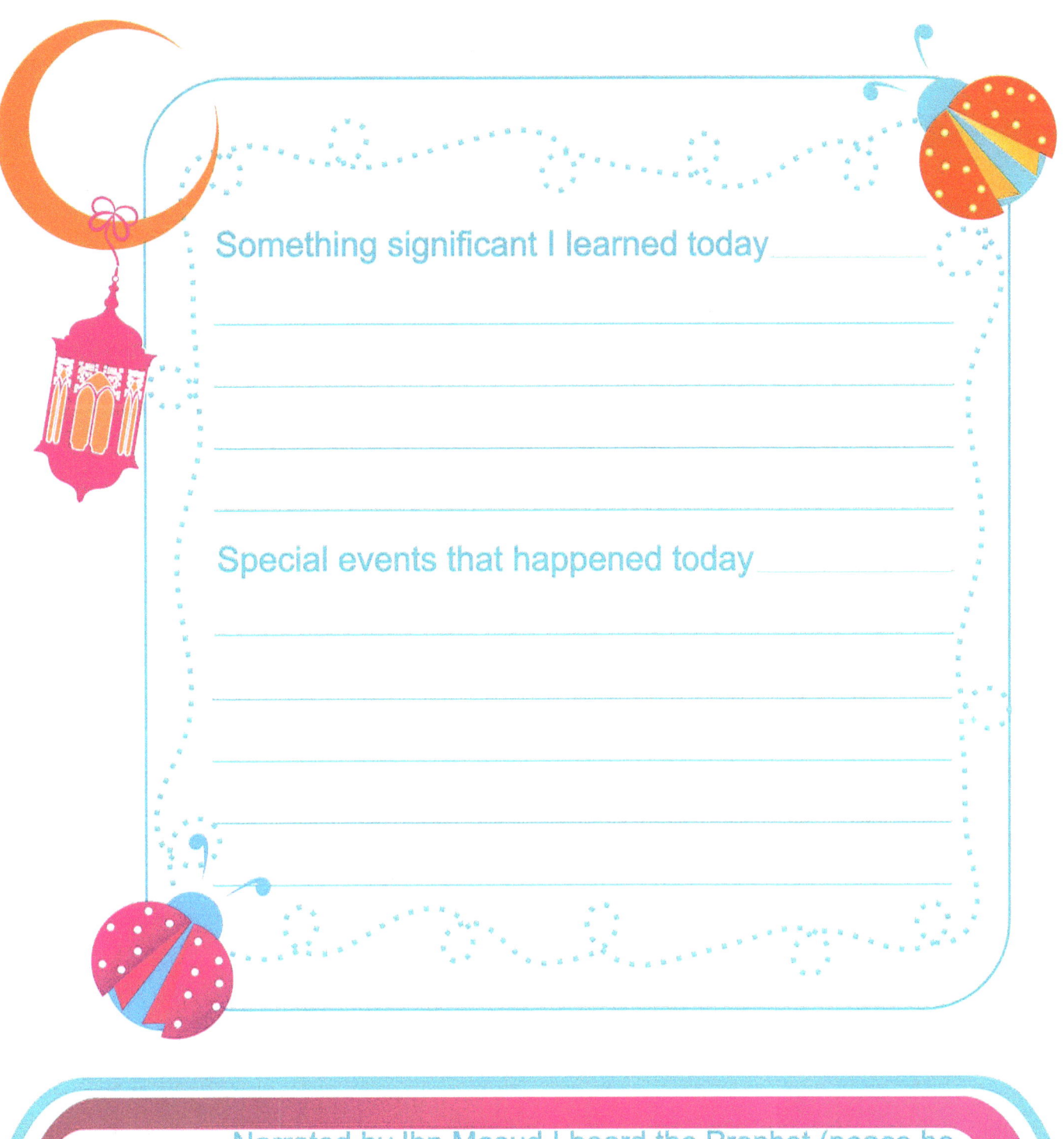

Allah's fogivness has no limits. No sin is too big for Allah to forgive,Ramadan is your chance to get all your previous sins forgiven.

Regardless of any sins you have committed in the past if you repent to Allah with sincerity He will accept your repentance and forgive your sins.

Don't forget to use the to do list in the next page to write down your main goals and dreams in these special days.

Fill these days with good deeds to erase any bad deeds you may have committed before.

A Wise, Young Muslim Boy

Many years ago, during the time of the Tabi'in (the generation of Muslims after the Sahabah), Baghdad was a great city of Islam. In fact, it was the capital of the Islamic Empire and, because of the great number of scholars who lived there, it was the center of Islamic knowledge. One day, the ruler of Rome at the time sent an envoy to Baghdad with three challenges for the Muslims. When the messenger reached the city, he informed the khalifah that he had three questions which he challenged the Muslims to answer.

The khalifah gathered together all the scholars of the city and the Roman messenger climbed upon a high platform and said, "I have come with three questions. If you answer them, then I will leave with you a great amount of wealth which I have brought from the king of Rome." As for the questions, they were:
"What was there before Allah?" "In which direction does Allah face?" "What is Allah engaged in at this moment?" The great assembly of people were silent. (Can you think of answers to these questions?)

In the midst of these brilliant scholars and students of Islam was a man looking on with his young son. "O my dear father! I will answer him and silence him!" said the youth. So the boy sought the permission of the khalifah to give the answers and he was given the permission to do so.
The Roman addressed the young Muslim and repeated his first question, "What was there before Allah?" The boy asked, "Do you know how to count?" "Yes," said the man. "Then count down from ten!" So the Roman counted down, "ten, nine, eight, ..." until he reached "one" and he stopped counting. "But what comes before 'one'?" asked the boy. "There is nothing before one- that is it!" said the man."Well then, if there obviously is nothing before the arithmetic 'one', then how do you expect that there should be anything
before the 'One' who is Absolute Truth, All-Eternal, Everlasting- the First, the Last,the Manifest, the Hidden?" Now the man was surprised by this direct answer which he could not dispute. So he asked, "Then tell me, in which direction is Allah facing?" "Bring a candle and light it," said the boy, "and tell me in which direction the flame is facing."

A Wise, Young Muslim Boy

"But the flame is just light- it spreads in each of the four directions- north, south, east and west. It does not face any one direction only," said the man in wonderment. The boy cried, "Then if this physical light spreads in all four directions such that you cannot tell me which way it faces, then what do you expect of the Nur-us-Samawati-wal-'Ard: Allah- the Light of the Heavens and the Earth!? Light upon light, Allah faces all directions at all times."

The Roman was stupefied and astounded that here was a young child answering his challenges in such a way that he could not argue against the proofs. So, he desperately wanted to try his final question. But before doing so, the boy said, "Wait! You are the one who is asking the questions and I am the one who is giving the answer to these challenges. It is only fair that you should come down to where I am standing and that I should go up where you are right now, in order that the answers may be heard as clearly as the questions." This seemed reasonable to the Roman, so he came down from where he was standing and the boy ascended the platform.

Then the man repeated his final challenge, "Tell me, what is Allah doing at this moment?" The boy proudly answered, "At this moment, when Allah found upon this high platform a liar and mocker of Islam, He caused him to descend and brought him low. And as for the one who believed in the Oneness of Allah, He raised him up and established the truth. "Every day He is in (i.e. bringing about) a matter.
(The Holy Quran 55:29)." The Roman had nothing to say except to leave and return back to his country, defeated.

Meanwhile, this young boy grew up to become one of the most famous scholars of Islam. Allah, the Exalted, blessed him with special wisdom and knowledge of the deen. His name was Abu Hanifah (rahmatullah 'alayhi- Allah have mercy on him) and he is known today as Imam-e-A'zam, the great imam and scholar of Islam. May Allah shower some of His Mercy in the same way upon our Muslim children who are growing up today. Ameen.

[Adapted into English from "Manaqib Abi Hanifah", written by Imam Muwaffaq Ibn Ahmad al-Makki (d. 568 Hijri). Dar al-Kitab al-'Arabiy, Beirut, 1981/1401H.]

Day 11 — Write down the main things you did in each area

Area				
Prayer	Obligatory prayers	Sunan prayers	Tarwaeeh prayers	Night prayers
Quran	Daily reading		Memorizing	
Duaa&zikr	Special duaa's for Ramadan	Morning&evening azkaar	Filling time with zikr	
Fasting	No food or drink	Dua'a at iftar	Keeping tongue pure	Iftar&suhoor at best times
Ethics	Honesty&integrity	Only saying good words	Helping others	Working hard
Parents	Obeying them	Putting a smile on their face	Helping around the house	
Relatives	Upholding continuous contact with them		Making them happy	
Siblings	Being cooperative&kind	Helping them out	Supporting&advising them	
Friends	Being cooperative&kind	Helping them out	Supporting&advising them	
Food	Not overeating	Eating healthy food	Break fast with 3 dates/water	
Exercise	Walking for 30 min daily		Performing sport activity 3 days a week	
Charity				

Areas I need to improve

_____
_____
_____
_____
_____
_____

Narrated by Abu Huraira: Allah's Apostle (peace be upon him) said, "Fasting is a shield (or a shelter). So, the person observing fasting should not behave foolishly and impudently, and if somebody fights with him or abuses him, he should tell him twice, "I am fasting." The Prophet added, "By Him in Whose Hands my soul is, the smell coming out from the mouth of a fasting person is better in the sight of Allah than the smell of musk. (Allah says about the fasting person), 'He has left his food, drink and desires for My sake. The fast is for Me. So I will reward (the fasting person) for it and the reward of good deeds is multiplied ten times."

Sahih Bukhari Book 31 Hadith 118

Day 12 — Write down the main things you did in each area

Area				
Prayer	Obligatory prayers	Sunan prayers	Tarwaeeh prayers	Night prayers
Quran	Daily reading		Memorizing	
Duaa&zikr	Special duaa's for Ramadan	Morning&evening azkaar	Filling time with zikr	
Fasting	No food or drink	Dua'a at iftar	Keeping tongue pure	Iftar&suhoor at best times
Ethics	Honesty&integrity	Only saying good words	Helping others	Working hard
Parents	Obeying them	Putting a smile on their face	Helping around the house	
Relatives	Upholding continuous contact with them	Making them happy		
Siblings	Being cooperative&kind	Helping them out	Supporting&advising them	
Friends	Being cooperative&kind	Helping them out	Supporting&advising them	
Food	Not overeating	Eating healthy food	Break fast with 3 dates/water	
Exercise	Walking for 30 min daily	Performing sport activity 3 days a week		
Charity				

Something significant I learned today

Special events that happened today

Abu Huraira reported Allah's Messenger (may peace be upon him) as saying: If anyone forgets that he is fasting and eats or drinks he should complete his fast, for it is only Allah Who has fed him and given him drink.

Sahih Muslim Book 6 Hadith 2575

Day 13 — Write down the main things you did in each area

Area				
Prayer	Obligatory prayers	Sunan prayers	Tarwaeeh prayers	Night prayers
Quran	Daily reading		Memorizing	
Duaa&zikr	Special duaa's for Ramadan	Morning&evening azkaar	Filling time with zikr	
Fasting	No food or drink	Dua'a at iftar	Keeping tongue pure	Iftar&suhoor at best times
Ethics	Honesty&integrity	Only saying good words	Helping others	Working hard
Parents	Obeying them	Putting a smile on their face	Helping around the house	
Relatives	Upholding continuous contact with them		Making them happy	
Siblings	Being cooperative&kind	Helping them out	Supporting&advising them	
Friends	Being cooperative&kind	Helping them out	Supporting&advising them	
Food	Not overeating	Eating healthy food	Break fast with 3 dates/water	
Exercise	Walking for 30 min daily		Performing sport activity 3 days a week	
Charity				

Areas I need to improve

_____
_____
_____
_____
_____

Narrated by Al-Walid bin 'Aizar I heard Abi Amr 'Ash-Shaibani saying, "The owner of this house." he pointed to 'Abdullah's house, "said, 'I asked the Prophet 'Which deed is loved most by Allah?" He replied, 'To offer prayers at their early (very first) stated times.' " 'Abdullah asked, "What is the next (in goodness)?" The Prophet said, "To be good and dutiful to one's parents," 'Abdullah asked, "What is the next (in goodness)?" The Prophet said, To participate in Jihad for Allah's Cause." 'Abdullah added, "The Prophet narrated to me these three things, and if I had asked more, he would have told me more."

Sahih Bukhari Book 73 Hadith 1

Day 14 — Write down the main things you did in each area

Area				
Prayer	Obligatory prayers	Sunan prayers	Tarwaeeh prayers	Night prayers
Quran	Daily reading		Memorizing	
Duaa&zikr	Special duaa's for Ramadan	Morning&evening azkaar		Filling time with zikr
Fasting	No food or drink	Dua'a at iftar	Keeping tongue pure	Iftar&suhoor at best times
Ethics	Honesty&integrity	Only saying good words	Helping others	Working hard
Parents	Obeying them	Putting a smile on their face	Helping around the house	
Relatives	Upholding continuous contact with them		Making them happy	
Siblings	Being cooperative&kind	Helping them out	Supporting&advising them	
Friends	Being cooperative&kind	Helping them out	Supporting&advising them	
Food	Not overeating	Eating healthy food	Break fast with 3 dates/water	
Exercise	Walking for 30 min daily		Performing sport activity 3 days a week	
Charity				

Something significant I learned today

_____
_____
_____
_____

Special events that happened today

_____
_____
_____
_____
_____

Anas related that the prophet (peace be upon him) said: Take the Suhoor meal, for there is blessing in it.

Sahih Bukhari and Muslim

Day 15 — Write down the main things you did in each area

Area				
Prayer	Obligatory prayers	Sunan prayers	Tarwaeeh prayers	Night prayers
Quran	Daily reading		Memorizing	
Duaa&zikr	Special duaa's for Ramadan	Morning&evening azkaar		Filling time with zikr
Fasting	No food or drink	Dua'a at iftar	Keeping tongue pure	Iftar&suhoor at best times
Ethics	Honesty&integrity	Only saying good words	Helping others	Working hard
Parents	Obeying them	Putting a smile on their face	Helping around the house	
Relatives	Upholding continuous contact with them		Making them happy	
Siblings	Being cooperative&kind	Helping them out	Supporting&advising them	
Friends	Being cooperative&kind	Helping them out	Supporting&advising them	
Food	Not overeating	Eating healthy food	Break fast with 3 dates/water	
Exercise	Walking for 30 min daily		Performing sport activity 3 days a week	
Charity				

Areas I need to improve

_____
_____
_____
_____
_____
_____

Narrated by An-Nu'man bin Bashir Allah's Apostle (may peace and blessings be upon him) said, "You see the believers as regards their being merciful among themselves and showing love among themselves and being kind, resembling one body, so that, if any part of the body is not well then the whole body shares the sleeplessness (insomnia) and fever with it."

Bukhari Book 73 Hadith 40

Day 16 — Write down the main things you did in each area

Area				
Prayer	Obligatory prayers	Sunan prayers	Tarwaeeh prayers	Night prayers
Quran	Daily reading		Memorizing	
Duaa&zikr	Special duaa's for Ramadan	Morning&evening azkaar	Filling time with zikr	
Fasting	No food or drink	Dua'a at iftar	Keeping tongue pure	Iftar&suhoor at best times
Ethics	Honesty&integrity	Only saying good words	Helping others	Working hard
Parents	Obeying them	Putting a smile on their face	Helping around the house	
Relatives	Upholding continuous contact with them		Making them happy	
Siblings	Being cooperative&kind	Helping them out	Supporting&advising them	
Friends	Being cooperative&kind	Helping them out	Supporting&advising them	
Food	Not overeating	Eating healthy food	Break fast with 3 dates/water	
Exercise	Walking for 30 min daily		Performing sport activity 3 days a week	
Charity				

Something significant I learned today

_____
_____
_____
_____

Special events that happened today

_____
_____
_____
_____
_____
_____

Narrated by Abu Huraira Allah's Apostle (peace be upon him) said, "Satan puts three knots at the back of the head of any of you if he is asleep. On every knot he reads and exhales the following words, 'The night is long, so stay asleep.' When one wakes up and remembers Allah, one knot is undone; and when one performs ablution, the second knot is undone, and when one prays the third knot is undone and one gets up energetic with a good heart in the morning; otherwise one gets up lazy and with a mischievous heart."

Sahih Bukhari Book 21 Number 243

Day 17 — Write down the main things you did in each area

Area				
Prayer	Obligatory prayers	Sunan prayers	Tarwaeeh prayers	Night prayers
Quran	Daily reading		Memorizing	
Duaa&zikr	Special duaa's for Ramadan	Morning&evening azkaar	Filling time with zikr	
Fasting	No food or drink	Dua'a at iftar	Keeping tongue pure	Iftar&suhoor at best times
Ethics	Honesty&integrity	Only saying good words	Helping others	Working hard
Parents	Obeying them	Putting a smile on their face	Helping around the house	
Relatives	Upholding continuous contact with them		Making them happy	
Siblings	Being cooperative&kind	Helping them out	Supporting&advising them	
Friends	Being cooperative&kind	Helping them out	Supporting&advising them	
Food	Not overeating	Eating healthy food	Break fast with 3 dates/water	
Exercise	Walking for 30 min daily		Performing sport activity 3 days a week	
Charity				

Areas I need to improve

_____
_____
_____
_____
_____
_____

Abu Huraira related that the Prophet (peace be upon him) said: Allah the Majestic and Exalted said: "Every deed of man will receive ten to 700 times reward, except Siyam (fasting), for it is for Me and I shall reward it (as I like). There are two occasions of joy for one who fasts: one when he breaks the fast and the other when he will meet his Lord".

Sahih Muslim Book 6 Hadith 2567

Day 18 — Write down the main things you did in each area

Area				
Prayer	Obligatory prayers	Sunan prayers	Tarwaeeh prayers	Night prayers
Quran	Daily reading		Memorizing	
Duaa&zikr	Special duaa's for Ramadan	Morning&evening azkaar	Filling time with zikr	
Fasting	No food or drink	Dua'a at iftar	Keeping tongue pure	Iftar&suhoor at best times
Ethics	Honesty&integrity	Only saying good words	Helping others	Working hard
Parents	Obeying them	Putting a smile on their face	Helping around the house	
Relatives	Upholding continuous contact with them	Making them happy		
Siblings	Being cooperative&kind	Helping them out	Supporting&advising them	
Friends	Being cooperative&kind	Helping them out	Supporting&advising them	
Food	Not overeating	Eating healthy food	Break fast with 3 dates/water	
Exercise	Walking for 30 min daily	Performing sport activity 3 days a week		
Charity				

Something significant I learned today

Special events that happened today

Narrated by Abu Huraira Allah's Apostle (peace be upon him) said, "When the month of Ramadan starts, the gates of the heaven are opened and the gates of Hell are closed and the devils are chained."

Sahih Bukhari Book 31 Hadith 123

Day 19 — Write down the main things you did in each area

Area				
Prayer	Obligatory prayers	Sunan prayers	Tarwaeeh prayers	Night prayers
Quran	Daily reading		Memorizing	
Duaa&zikr	Special duaa's for Ramadan	Morning&evening azkaar		Filling time with zikr
Fasting	No food or drink	Dua'a at iftar	Keeping tongue pure	Iftar&suhoor at best times
Ethics	Honesty&integrity	Only saying good words	Helping others	Working hard
Parents	Obeying them	Putting a smile on their face	Helping around the house	
Relatives	Upholding continuous contact with them		Making them happy	
Siblings	Being cooperative&kind	Helping them out	Supporting&advising them	
Friends	Being cooperative&kind	Helping them out	Supporting&advising them	
Food	Not overeating	Eating healthy food	Break fast with 3 dates/water	
Exercise	Walking for 30 min daily		Performing sport activity 3 days a week	
Charity				

Areas I need to improve

_____
_____
_____
_____
_____
_____

Narrated by Abu Huraira: A man came to the Prophet and asked, "O Allah's Apostle! Which charity is the most superior in reward?" He replied, "The charity which you practice while you are healthy, and afraid of poverty and wish to become wealthy. Do not delay it to the time of approaching death and then say, 'Give so much to such and such, and so much to such and such.' And it has already belonged to such and such (as it is too late)."

Sahih Bukhari Book 24 Hadith 500

Day 20 — Write down the main things you did in each area

Area				
Prayer	Obligatory prayers	Sunan prayers	Tarwaeeh prayers	Night prayers
Quran	Daily reading		Memorizing	
Duaa&zikr	Special duaa's for Ramadan	Morning&evening azkaar		Filling time with zikr
Fasting	No food or drink	Dua'a at iftar	Keeping tongue pure	Iftar&suhoor at best times
Ethics	Honesty&integrity	Only saying good words	Helping others	Working hard
Parents	Obeying them	Putting a smile on their face	Helping around the house	
Relatives	Upholding continuous contact with them		Making them happy	
Siblings	Being cooperative&kind	Helping them out	Supporting&advising them	
Friends	Being cooperative&kind	Helping them out	Supporting&advising them	
Food	Not overeating	Eating healthy food	Break fast with 3 dates/water	
Exercise	Walking for 30 min daily		Performing sport activity 3 days a week	
Charity				

Something significant I learned today

Special events that happened today

Salman ibn Amir Dhabi related that the Prophet (peace be upon him) said: Break your fast with dates, or else with water, for it is purifier.

Sahih Bukhari and Muslim

The last ten nights of Ramadan are very special. These are the nights that the Prophet Muhammad (peace be upon him) would spend in constant worship. Among these nights is Laylat al-Qadr (the Night of Power) – a night more blessed than a thousand months.

The Prophet (peace be upon him) used to single these nights out for worship and the performance of good deeds. He would exert himself in worship during these ten nights more than any other nights of the year. Work the hardest you can in these days as their blessings will last you in this life and the next.

Don't forget to use the to do list in the next page to write down your main goals and dreams in these special days.

It's forbidden

It is forbidden to kill one another,
Yet here we are killing our sisters and brothers.
By our silence we are condemning them to death
Where are we when they take their last breath?
Like lambs to the slaughter we're being led
Too frightened to do anything except nod our heads
By our own hands our traditions and religion goes
By our silence we're selling our souls
Where are the strong Muslims of old?
Who to Allah's words they would strongly hold
When an attack on one was an attack on all
No injustice was left no matter how small
When the rich would give to the needy and poor
And there was protection and justice for all
Nor was there killing of innocent women and children
Terrorism is not the Islamic religion
When all Muslims stood proud and strong as one nation
And Islam stood for peace, justice and protection
United we stood strong and tall
But now disjointed we are beginning to crumble and fall
Speak out; use your voice we can all do more
Show the world what Islam truly stands for.

By Aisha Abdel Rahman

The Night of Power

On the night of power, the blessed night
Man was sent a guiding light
To lead man off their path of destruction
Onto a path of eternal salvation
A final message, a final guide
A universal message of mercy for all mankind
Revealed by Allah through divine inspiration
To our blessed prophet, Mohammed (May peace be upon him)
A book of knowledge, teaching and instruction
Of life, science and of wisdom
Delve into its passages and a treasure you will find
As the doors of life's mysteries are thrown open wide.
Reasons for man's existence and creation
Answers to all man's many questions
Unveiled is a perfect law of life
Rules when followed bring us from darkness to light
A warning to those who choose to pursue evil
Of Hell's ferocious fire if they follow the Devil
A beautiful message for those who follow Allah's words
Eternal Paradise will be their reward
Good news to those who accept its guidance
Of forgiveness, purification and salvation
So powerful that it can move mountains
Preserved in purity, eternally guarded from corruption
This is the Qur'an Allah's blessed gift to us The key to eternal Paradise.

By Aisha Abdel Rahman

Day 21 — Write down the main things you did in each area

Area				
Prayer	Obligatory prayers	Sunan prayers	Tarwaeeh prayers	Night prayers
Quran	Daily reading		Memorizing	
Duaa&zikr	Special duaa's for Ramadan	Morning&evening azkaar	Filling time with zikr	
Fasting	No food or drink	Dua'a at iftar	Keeping tongue pure	Iftar&suhoor at best times
Ethics	Honesty&integrity	Only saying good words	Helping others	Working hard
Parents	Obeying them	Putting a smile on their face	Helping around the house	
Relatives	Upholding continuous contact with them		Making them happy	
Siblings	Being cooperative&kind	Helping them out	Supporting&advising them	
Friends	Being cooperative&kind	Helping them out	Supporting&advising them	
Food	Not overeating	Eating healthy food	Break fast with 3 dates/water	
Exercise	Walking for 30 min daily		Performing sport activity 3 days a week	
Charity				

Something significant I learned today

_____
_____
_____
_____
_____
_____

Abû Ayyûb al-Ansârî relates that Allah's Messenger (peace be upon him) says: "Whoever fasts the month of Ramadan and then follows it with six days of fasting in the month of Shawwâl, it will be as if he had fasted the year through."

Reported by Sahîh Muslim Hadith 1163

Day 22 — Write down the main things you did in each area

Area				
Prayer	Obligatory prayers	Sunan prayers	Tarwaeeh prayers	Night prayers
Quran	Daily reading		Memorizing	
Duaa&zikr	Special duaa's for Ramadan	Morning&evening azkaar		Filling time with zikr
Fasting	No food or drink	Dua'a at iftar	Keeping tongue pure	Iftar&suhoor at best times
Ethics	Honesty&integrity	Only saying good words	Helping others	Working hard
Parents	Obeying them	Putting a smile on their face	Helping around the house	
Relatives	Upholding continuous contact with them		Making them happy	
Siblings	Being cooperative&kind	Helping them out	Supporting&advising them	
Friends	Being cooperative&kind	Helping them out	Supporting&advising them	
Food	Not overeating	Eating healthy food	Break fast with 3 dates/water	
Exercise	Walking for 30 min daily		Performing sport activity 3 days a week	
Charity				

Areas I need to improve

_____
_____
_____
_____
_____
_____

"Abu Huraira narrated that the Prophet (may peace be upon him) commanded the person (who) broke the fast in Ramadan without a valid reason to free a slave or observe fasts for two (consecutive) months or feed sixty poor persons."

Sahih Bukhari Book 6 Hadith 2461

Day 23 — Write down the main things you did in each area

Area				
Prayer	Obligatory prayers	Sunan prayers	Tarwaeeh prayers	Night prayers
Quran	Daily reading		Memorizing	
Duaa&zikr	Special duaa's for Ramadan	Morning&evening azkaar		Filling time with zikr
Fasting	No food or drink	Dua'a at iftar	Keeping tongue pure	Iftar&suhoor at best times
Ethics	Honesty&integrity	Only saying good words	Helping others	Working hard
Parents	Obeying them	Putting a smile on their face	Helping around the house	
Relatives	Upholding continuous contact with them		Making them happy	
Siblings	Being cooperative&kind	Helping them out	Supporting&advising them	
Friends	Being cooperative&kind	Helping them out	Supporting&advising them	
Food	Not overeating	Eating healthy food	Break fast with 3 dates/water	
Exercise	Walking for 30 min daily		Performing sport activity 3 days a week	
Charity				

Something significant I learned today

_____
_____
_____
_____
_____
_____

"Verily, We have sent it (this Qur'an) down in the Night of Al Qadr. And what will make you know what the Night of Al Qadr is? The Night of Al Qadr is better than a thousand months (i.e. worshipping Allah in that night is better than worshipping Him a thousand months, i.e. 83 years and 4 months). Therein descend the angels and the Rooh [Jibreel (Gabriel)] by Allah's Permission with all Decrees, (All that night), there is peace (and goodness from Allah to His believing slaves) until the appearance of dawn."

The Holy Quran Chpater 97 verses 1:5

Day 24 — Write down the main things you did in each area

Area				
Prayer	Obligatory prayers	Sunan prayers	Tarwaeeh prayers	Night prayers
Quran	Daily reading		Memorizing	
Duaa&zikr	Special duaa's for Ramadan	Morning&evening azkaar		Filling time with zikr
Fasting	No food or drink	Dua'a at iftar	Keeping tongue pure	Iftar&suhoor at best times
Ethics	Honesty&integrity	Only saying good words	Helping others	Working hard
Parents	Obeying them	Putting a smile on their face	Helping around the house	
Relatives	Upholding continuous contact with them		Making them happy	
Siblings	Being cooperative&kind	Helping them out	Supporting&advising them	
Friends	Being cooperative&kind	Helping them out	Supporting&advising them	
Food	Not overeating	Eating healthy food	Break fast with 3 dates/water	
Exercise	Walking for 30 min daily		Performing sport activity 3 days a week	
Charity				

Areas I need to improve

_____
_____
_____
_____
_____
_____

"Abu Hurayrah narrated that the Prophet (peace be upon him) said: "Whoever stays up and prays on Laylat al-Qadr out of faith and in the hope of reward, his previous sins will be forgiven."
Sahih Bukhari and Muslim

Day 25 — Write down the main things you did in each area

Area				
Prayer	Obligatory prayers	Sunan prayers	Tarwaeeh prayers	Night prayers
Quran	Daily reading		Memorizing	
Duaa&zikr	Special duaa's for Ramadan	Morning&evening azkaar	Filling time with zikr	
Fasting	No food or drink	Dua'a at iftar	Keeping tongue pure	Iftar&suhoor at best times
Ethics	Honesty&integrity	Only saying good words	Helping others	Working hard
Parents	Obeying them	Putting a smile on their face	Helping around the house	
Relatives	Upholding continuous contact with them		Making them happy	
Siblings	Being cooperative&kind	Helping them out	Supporting&advising them	
Friends	Being cooperative&kind	Helping them out	Supporting&advising them	
Food	Not overeating	Eating healthy food	Break fast with 3 dates/water	
Exercise	Walking for 30 min daily		Performing sport activity 3 days a week	
Charity				

Something significant I learned today

_____
_____
_____
_____
_____
_____

'A'ishah (may Allah be pleased with her) narrated that the Prophet (peace be upon him) used to strive hard (in worship) during the last ten days of Ramadan in a way that he did not strive at any other time.

Sahih Muslim, hadith 1175

Day 26 — Write down the main things you did in each area

Area				
Prayer	Obligatory prayers	Sunan prayers	Tarwaeeh prayers	Night prayers
Quran	Daily reading		Memorizing	
Duaa&zikr	Special duaa's for Ramadan	Morning&evening azkaar		Filling time with zikr
Fasting	No food or drink	Dua'a at iftar	Keeping tongue pure	Iftar&suhoor at best times
Ethics	Honesty&integrity	Only saying good words	Helping others	Working hard
Parents	Obeying them	Putting a smile on their face	Helping around the house	
Relatives	Upholding continuous contact with them		Making them happy	
Siblings	Being cooperative&kind	Helping them out	Supporting&advising them	
Friends	Being cooperative&kind	Helping them out	Supporting&advising them	
Food	Not overeating	Eating healthy food	Break fast with 3 dates/water	
Exercise	Walking for 30 min daily		Performing sport activity 3 days a week	
Charity				

Areas I need to improve

_____
_____
_____
_____
_____
_____

It is reported from the hadith of 'A'ishah (may Allah be pleased with her) that when the last ten days of Ramadan came, the Prophet (peace be upon him) would stay up at night, wake his family and gird his loins.
  Sahih Bukhari and Muslim.
Her phrase "girded his loins" is a metaphor for his preparing himself to worship and strive hard in worship.

Day 27 — Write down the main things you did in each area

Area				
Prayer	Obligatory prayers	Sunan prayers	Tarwaeeh prayers	Night prayers
Quran	Daily reading		Memorizing	
Duaa&zikr	Special duaa's for Ramadan	Morning&evening azkaar		Filling time with zikr
Fasting	No food or drink	Dua'a at iftar	Keeping tongue pure	Iftar&suhoor at best times
Ethics	Honesty&integrity	Only saying good words	Helping others	Working hard
Parents	Obeying them	Putting a smile on their face	Helping around the house	
Relatives	Upholding continuous contact with them		Making them happy	
Siblings	Being cooperative&kind	Helping them out	Supporting&advising them	
Friends	Being cooperative&kind	Helping them out	Supporting&advising them	
Food	Not overeating	Eating healthy food	Break fast with 3 dates/water	
Exercise	Walking for 30 min daily		Performing sport activity 3 days a week	
Charity				

Something significant I learned today

_____
_____
_____
_____
_____

'A'ishah (may Allah be pleased with her) reported that she said: "O Messenger of Allah! What if I knew which night Lailatul-Qadr was, then what should I say in it?" He said 'Say

اَللّٰهُمَّ اِنَّكَ عَفُوٌّ، تُحِبُّ الْعَفْوَ فَاعْفُ عَنِّي

(Allahuma innakka 'Affuwan tuhibbu l-'afwa fa'fu 'anni) O Allah You are The One Who pardons greatly, and loves to pardon, so pardon me.

Day 28 — Write down the main things you did in each area

Area				
Prayer	Obligatory prayers	Sunan prayers	Tarwaeeh prayers	Night prayers
Quran	Daily reading		Memorizing	
Duaa&zikr	Special duaa's for Ramadan	Morning&evening azkaar	Filling time with zikr	
Fasting	No food or drink	Dua'a at iftar	Keeping tongue pure	Iftar&suhoor at best times
Ethics	Honesty&integrity	Only saying good words	Helping others	Working hard
Parents	Obeying them	Putting a smile on their face	Helping around the house	
Relatives	Upholding continuous contact with them		Making them happy	
Siblings	Being cooperative&kind	Helping them out	Supporting&advising them	
Friends	Being cooperative&kind	Helping them out	Supporting&advising them	
Food	Not overeating	Eating healthy food	Break fast with 3 dates/water	
Exercise	Walking for 30 min daily		Performing sport activity 3 days a week	
Charity				

Areas I need to improve

'A'ishah (may Allah be pleased with her) narrated that the Messenger of Allah (peace be upon him) said: "Seek Laylat al-Qadr in the odd-numbered nights of the last ten nights."

Sahih Bukhari, Book 4 Hadith 259

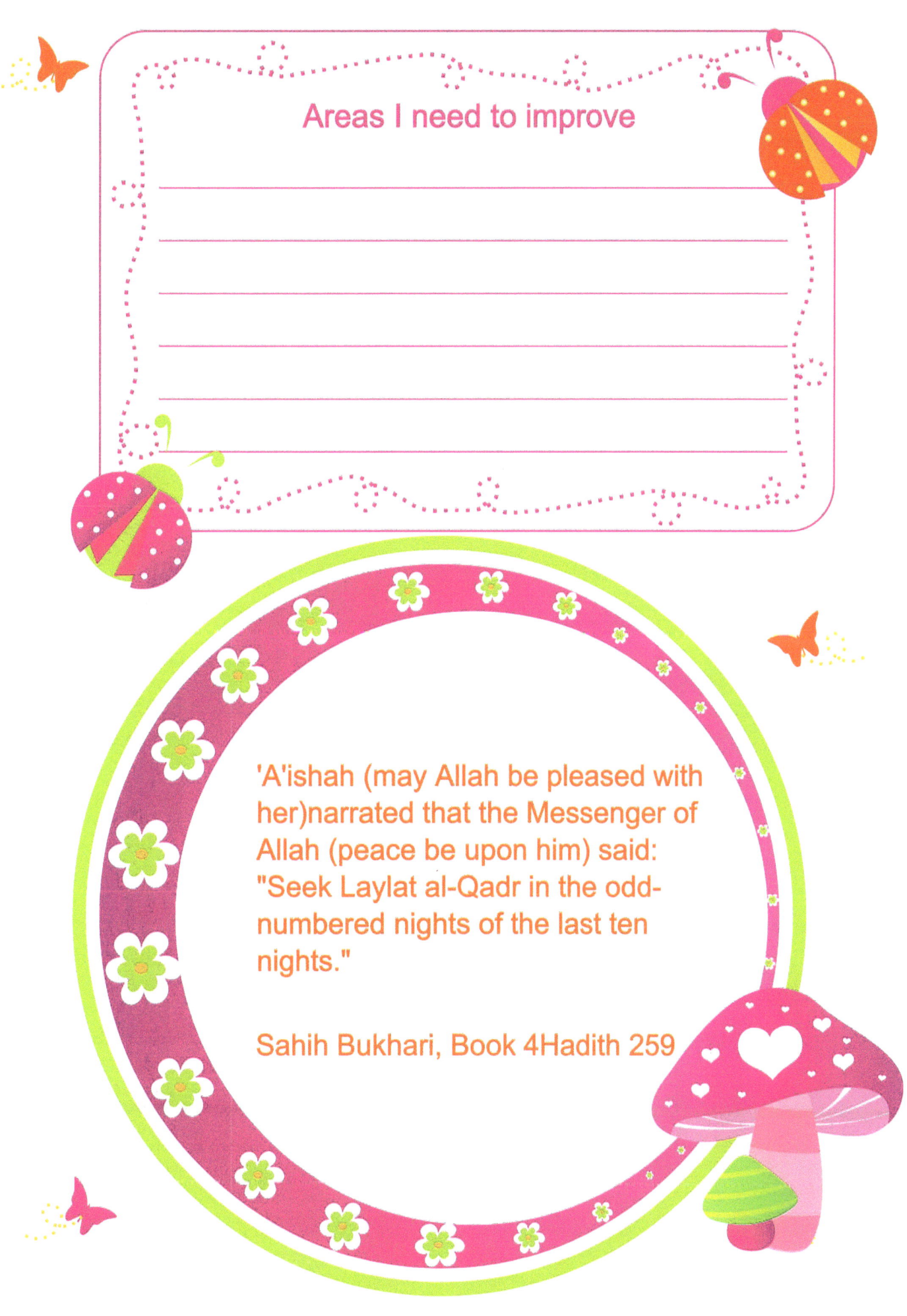

Day 29 — Write down the main things you did in each area

Area				
Prayer	Obligatory prayers	Sunan prayers	Tarwaeeh prayers	Night prayers
Quran	Daily reading		Memorizing	
Duaa&zikr	Special duaa's for Ramadan	Morning&evening azkaar	Filling time with zikr	
Fasting	No food or drink	Dua'a at iftar	Keeping tongue pure	Iftar&suhoor at best times
Ethics	Honesty&integrity	Only saying good words	Helping others	Working hard
Parents	Obeying them	Putting a smile on their face	Helping around the house	
Relatives	Upholding continuous contact with them		Making them happy	
Siblings	Being cooperative&kind	Helping them out	Supporting&advising them	
Friends	Being cooperative&kind	Helping them out	Supporting&advising them	
Food	Not overeating	Eating healthy food	Break fast with 3 dates/water	
Exercise	Walking for 30 min daily		Performing sport activity 3 days a week	
Charity				

Something significant I learned today

_____
_____
_____
_____
_____
_____

Narrated by Abu Huraira Allah's Apostle (peace be upon him) said, "The one who looks after and works for a widow and for a poor person is like a warrior fighting for Allah's Cause."

Sahih Bukhari, Book 73 Hadith 36

Day 30 — Write down the main things you did in each area

Area				
Prayer	Obligatory prayers	Sunan prayers	Tarwaeeh prayers	Night prayers
Quran	Daily reading		Memorizing	
Duaa&zikr	Special duaa's for Ramadan	Morning&evening azkaar	Filling time with zikr	
Fasting	No food or drink	Dua'a at iftar	Keeping tongue pure	Iftar&suhoor at best times
Ethics	Honesty&integrity	Only saying good words	Helping others	Working hard
Parents	Obeying them	Putting a smile on their face	Helping around the house	
Relatives	Upholding continuous contact with them		Making them happy	
Siblings	Being cooperative&kind	Helping them out	Supporting&advising them	
Friends	Being cooperative&kind	Helping them out	Supporting&advising them	
Food	Not overeating	Eating healthy food	Break fast with 3 dates/water	
Exercise	Walking for 30 min daily		Performing sport activity 3 days a week	
Charity				

Areas I need to improve

_____
_____
_____
_____
_____
_____

Ibn 'Umar reported that the Messenger of Allah (may peace be upon him) ordered that the Sadaqat-ul-Fitr should be paid before the people go out for prayer.

Sahih Muslim, Book 5 Hadith 2159

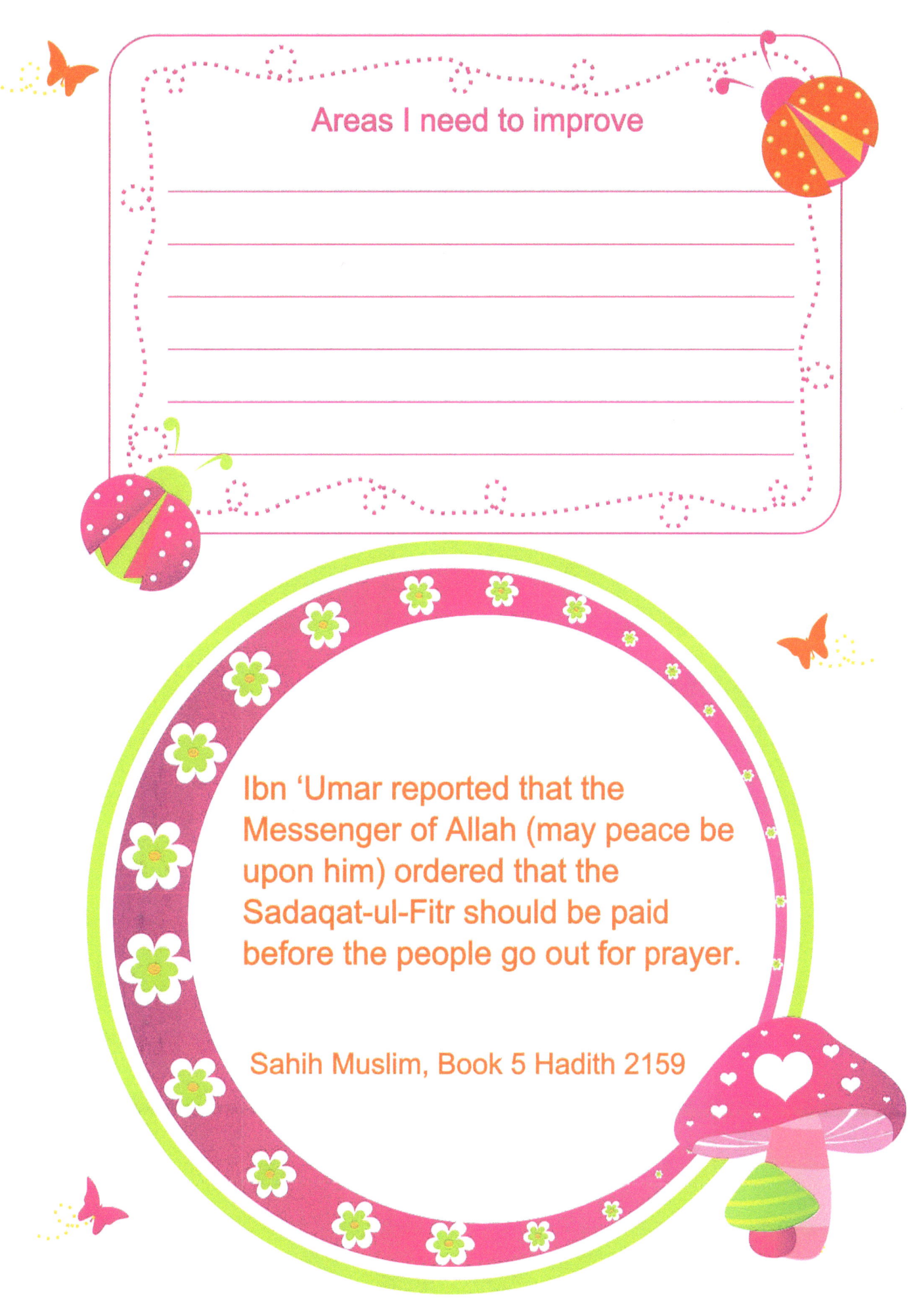

Allah's love

I was dust you gave me life
You gave me shape and form
With a garment of skin you clothed my bones
You breathed in me a soul
You gave me eyes so I may see your many wondrous things
And ears so I may hear nature as it sings
Limbs so I can walk and run upon your land
A brain so I may reason, think and understand
A heart so I can feel and know what's right from wrong
All these you gave to me wanting nothing in return
If I feel lost and in despair
I reach out and find you there
Through life's journey you are my guide
Protecting, comforting me, always by my side
You give me strength when I am weak
Light when times are dark and bleak
And though I hurt and let you down
Your mercy and forgiveness have no bounds
Your love is unconditional no matter what I do
Nobody could love me the way that you do

Allah's love

All living creation comes from your love
And shares your loving care,
Your love encompasses us, surrounds us everywhere
No soul that turns to you do you forsake
No request or plea do you not undertake
Always leading, guiding man, to their destiny
To live with you in Paradise for eternity
Vigilant, watching, always awake
Patiently, silently you wait
For man to worship and show their love for you
In the ways that you showed us to do

By Aisha Abdel Rahman

Eid is a blessed time and it's a celebration for all Muslims for having completed the month of fasting and worship.

Make sure to have fun in eid but to do it in ways that please Allah. Do not throw away all your hard work all Ramadan by comitting sins in eid. And make sure you go to the eid prayer as it is the sunnah of our beloved prophet (peace and blessings be upon him).

Treat this eid as a new begining that will hopefully change your life to the better and bring you closer to Allah and what you want to acheive in life.

Use the next page to make plans to make this eid a special one for you and your family.

Happy eid!

Halah Azim
My Ramadan plan - Gateway to paradise

© 2014, Halah Azim
www.theheartsoflight.com

About the author: Halah Azim is a British/Egyptian Muslim living in Australia. She has a B.A in computer engineering from Cairo and she also completed a 2 year diploma in Islamic studies from Cairo. Currently she is working on her B.A in extensive Islamic studies from the Islamic Online University.

To get more unique Islamic products for the whole family visit: www.theheartsoflight.com and make sure to join us on facebook, www.facebook.com/TheHeartsOfLight

ALL RIGHTS RESERVED. This book contains material protected under International and Federal Copyright Laws and Treaties. Any unauthorized reprint or use of this material is prohibited. No part of this book may be reproduced or transmitted in any form or by any means, electronic or mechanical, including photocopying, recording, or by any information storage and retrieval system without express written permission from the author.

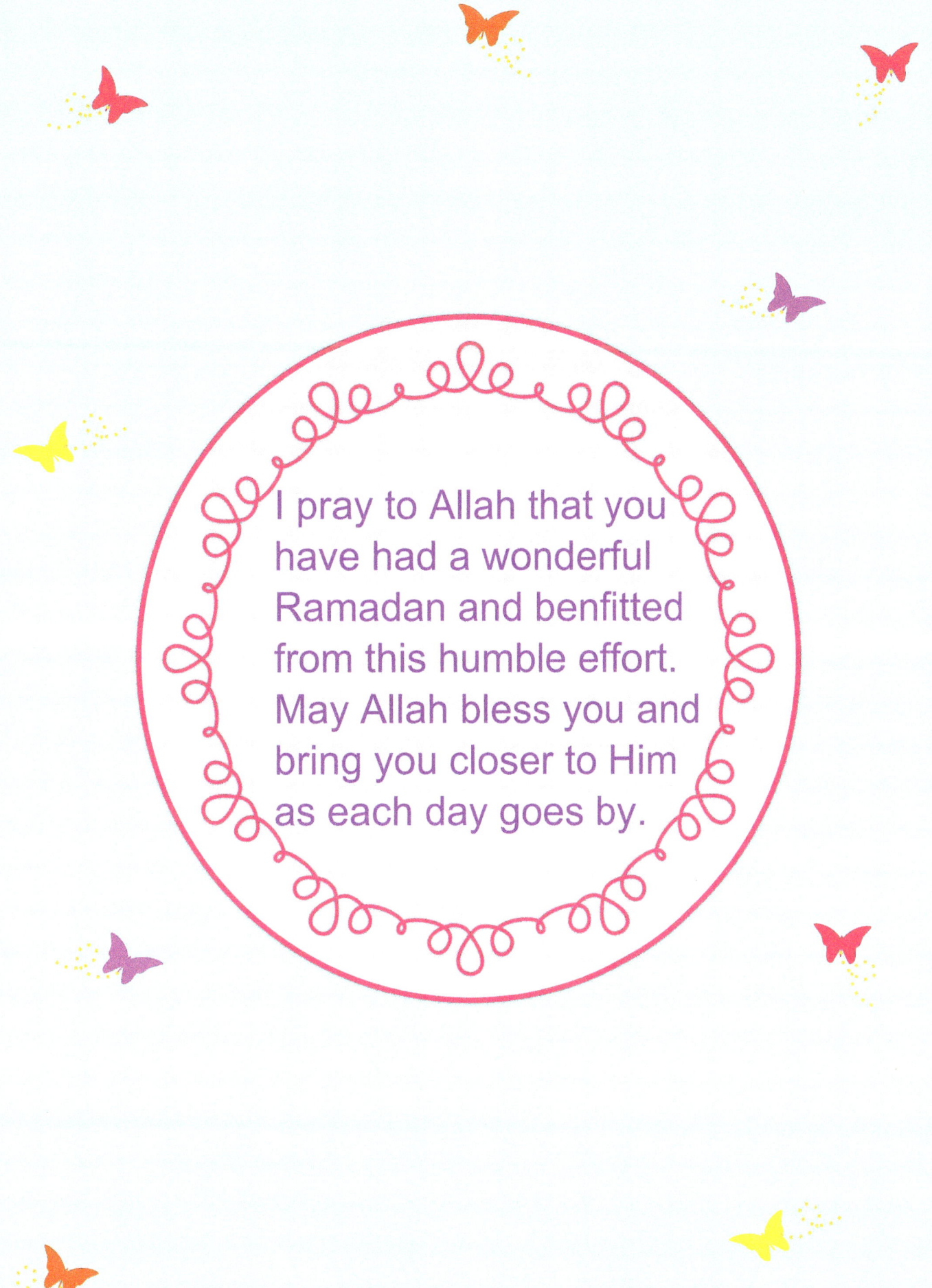

I pray to Allah that you have had a wonderful Ramadan and benfitted from this humble effort. May Allah bless you and bring you closer to Him as each day goes by.

www.ingramcontent.com/pod-product-compliance
Lightning Source LLC
Chambersburg PA
CBHW061814290426
44110CB00026B/2871